Emma Ewing

Vegetables and Vegetable Cooking

Emma Ewing

Vegetables and Vegetable Cooking

ISBN/EAN: 9783744788960

Printed in Europe, USA, Canada, Australia, Japan

Cover: Foto ©Lupo / pixelio.de

More available books at **www.hansebooks.com**

Cookery Manuals.

No. 4.

VEGETABLES and VEGETABLE COOKING.

BY

MRS. EMMA P. EWING.

CHICAGO:
FAIRBANKS, PALMER & CO.

1884.

TABLE OF CONTENTS.

VEGETABLES AND VEGETABLE COOKING.

PRELIMINARY REMARKS.

Market gardening is becoming so important an industry that the production of vegetables is rapidly on the increase. Many different kinds are already in general cultivation, others are being introduced to popular notice, and nearly all of them when cooked according to the best methods, are highly relished by a majority of people.

The cooking of vegetables is, however, so imperfectly understood, that instead of an attractive variety of them being served regularly at the average dinner table, it is not infrequently the case that the vegetable family is represented there, day after day, by the potato alone—and that always dressed in the same unvarying style.

The general rules applicable to the cooking of meats, etc., are also applicable to the cooking of vegetables, and they can only be cooked according to the seven primary methods, namely : Roasting, Baking, Boiling, Steaming, Stewing, Frying and Broiling; but the methods of seasoning, combining and serving may be varied so as to produce an almost limitless number of dishes with distinctive names.

A difference of opinion exists in regard to the temperature of the water in which different vegetables should be put to cook; but a safe general rule to follow, until the question is settled beyond all controversy, is:— To put all fresh or green vegetables in slightly salted boiling water, and let them cook gently until tender;—and to put all dried, leguminous vegetables, such as beans, peas, etc, in cold water, and after it reaches the boiling point, allow them to simmer gently until done.

Dried vegetables should be well soaked in cold water before they are cooked, and most green vegetables are improved by being subjected to the same process,— especially is this the case with potatoes, turnips, parsnips, salsify, etc., all of which become discolored, when pared or scraped, unless immediately laid in cold water.

For the sake of preserving them in handsome shape vegetables are often served under-done; but are more frequently sent to table an over-cooked, insipid mess. In either case they are unpalatable, indigestible and innutritious. They should always be cooked thoroughly, but never so much as to render them mushy, or cause them to tumble to pieces.

The length of time required for cooking any variety of vegetable depends greatly on its maturity or age, and varies considerably at different seasons. The time in which various vegetables will cook is approximated in the table here given; but the true, and only safe, rule is to test them occasionally during the process of cooking.

TIME TABLE.

Giving the approximate length of time required for cooking different vegetables :

30 MINUTES.—Asparagus, corn, macaroni, mushrooms, peas, boiled potatoes, tomatoes, lettuce.

45 MINUTES.—Young beets, carrots, parsnips, turnips, baked potatoes, rice.

ONE HOUR.—Artichokes, new cabbage, string beans, brussels sprouts, cauliflower, greens, salsify, new onions, winter squash.

TWO HOURS.—Winter cabbage, carrots, parsnips, turnips and onions.

THREE TO FIVE HOURS.—Old beets.

FIVE TO EIGHT HOURS.—Dried beans, dried peas, hominy, etc.

The flavor of vegetables can be very perfectly developed by the addition of suitable condiments, at the proper stage of their preparation for the table, and may, by judicious seasoning be modified to suit every taste.

Melted butter, drawn butter, clear sauce, white sauce, brown sauce, tomato sauce, and several salad dressings are appropriate for serving with different vegetables, or with the same vegetable prepared in different ways, and sugar, lemon juice, vinegar, salt, pepper

and numerous other spices are suitable seasonings fo many of them.

It is, however, impossible to give a specific recipe, of any practical value, in regard to the proper quantity of seasoning or dressing to be used with different vegetables, as some people like very little and others a great deal, consequently the matter must in a great measure, be left to individual judgment.

DRAWN BUTTER.

Cook together one ounce of flour and two ounces of butter—or about two measures of flour to one measure of butter—stirring meanwhile, until well mixed, add one pint of water or broth, boil until the flour is perfectly cooked and the sauce smooth, which will be in from two to five minutes, then season to taste with salt and pepper.

CLEAR SAUCE.

Cut meat, or meat and bone in small pieces, cover with cold water, add a little salt, simmer three or four hours, strain, and remove the grease.

WHITE SAUCE.

Cook together one ounce of flour and two ounces of butter, add one pint of sweet cream or milk, simmer gently five minutes, and season to taste with salt and pepper. When desired acid, add lemon juice or vinegar just before serving.

BROWN SAUCE.

Cook together one ounce of flour and two ounces of butter, stirring constantly, until a dark brown, add a pint of cold water or broth, cook, and season to taste with salt and pepper. By browning meat and making it into broth, a rich coloring can be obtained for brown sauce.

TOMATO SAUCE.

Stew a quart of tomatoes in a pint of any simple broth, or in their own juice, until very soft, rub through a sieve, and season to taste with salt and red pepper. If too acid, add a quarter of a teaspooonful of sugar.

FRENCH SALAD DRESSING.

To a half teaspoonful of made mustard add olive oil, stirring constantly until thick; then thin by adding vinegar in like manner; and thus alternate until the required quantity is obtained, when season to taste with salt and pepper. A French dressing, without mustard, is made by mixing together four teaspoonfuls of vinegar, half a teaspoonful of salt and one-eighth of a teaspoonful of pepper, and when used, adding olive oil.

CREAM DRESSING.

Cook together, two minutes, an ounce each of flour and butter, add a pint of sweet cream, and season with salt and pepper.

COOKED MAYONNAISE DRESSING.

To each table spoonful of boiling vinegar used, add the well beaten yolk of an egg, and cook in a bowl set in a pan of boiling water, till stiff. Remove from the fire, add an ounce of butter, and stir until cool and perfectly stiff. After it becomes cold season with salt, pepper and mustard, and thin to the required consistency with sweet cream.

VEGETABLES.

ARTICHOKE SALAD.

There are two kinds of artichokes—the Jerusalem and the Globe—both of which are occasionally served as salads. The former is a tuber, similar in appearance to a potato, and the latter a plant resembling a thistle, with a large scaly head, the under part only of which is edible. When eaten raw they are dressed according to taste, with melted butter or oil, and salt, pepper, mustard, vinegar, etc.

BOILED ARTICHOKES.

Wash and scrape Jerusalem artichokes, boil till tender, drain, and serve with drawn butter or white sauce, or mash fine and season with salt and pepper.

SCALLOPED ARTICHOKES.

Boil and mash Jerusalem artichokes, season with salt and pepper, put in shells, or in a baking dish, sprinkle with bread crumbs, moisten with butter, and brown in the oven.

FRIED ARTICHOKES.

Boil Globe artichokes, remove the chokes, divide the bottoms in pieces the size desired, dip in beaten egg and crumbs, and fry in butter or drippings.

BOILED ASPARAGUS.

Wash, tie in small bundles, cook till tender and serve on toast, with melted butter, or white sauce.

ASPARAGUS PEAS.

Wash, cut in small pieces, simmer till tender in just enough of water to cover, thicken slightly with flour and butter stirred together, add a little sweet cream, and season with salt and pepper.

ASPARAGUS ROLLS.

Cut cold boiled asparagus very fine, mix with beaten egg in a sauce pan, thicken with a little flour and milk stirred together, season with salt and pepper, pour hot into rolls from which the crumb has been removed and serve; or pour on toast and serve.

ASPARAGUS PUDDING.

Mix together half a pint of asparagus **peas**, **four** eggs, a table spoonful of finely minced ham, an ounce of butter, two table spoonfuls of flour, and milk sufficient to make a thick batter. Pour into a buttered pudding mould, steam two hours, and serve with drawn butter.

BOILED BEETS.

Wash, boil till tender, rub off the skin, slice and season with salt, pepper and melted butter.

STEWED BEETS.

Wash, parboil, rub off the skin, cut in slices, put in a stew pan, cover with milk, add a lump of butter rolled in flour, simmer till tender, and season with salt and pepper.

BAKED BEETS.

Bake in a moderate oven till tender, rub off the skins, baste with melted butter and lemon juice, put in the oven a few minutes, and serve hot.

BEET SALAD.

Mix equal quantities of boiled sliced beet and boiled sliced potato, and serve with cream dressing; or mix with onions, celery, endive and other vegetables, and serve with a French dressing.

STRING BEANS.

Remove the strings, put the beans in a small quantity of water—just enough to cover them—simmer gently till tender, drain, and serve with melted butter, or white sauce. Or break in small pieces, cook in a small quantity of water, let the water evaporate as the beans become sufficiently cooked, then add sweet cream, and season with salt and pepper.

SHELLED BEANS.

Put the beans in just sufficient water to cover them, stew gently till tender, add a little sweet cream, and season with salt and pepper; or omit the cream, and season with salt, pepper and butter.

DRIED BEANS.

Soak, put to cook in a liberal supply of cold water, which must be poured off as soon as it boils and enough of cold water to barely cover the beans be added, salt lightly, cook gently until very tender, but not falling to pieces, and season with salt, pepper and butter; or serve with white, or brown sauce.

BAKED BEANS.

Put a piece of salt pork and a little molasses in a bean pot, or a deep stone jar, and fill to within three inches of the top with beans that have been boiled until the skins will crack when exposed to cold air, and pour in enough of the water in which they were cooked to cover them. Place the lid on the jar, set it in the oven and bake from 6 to 12 hours—adding water occasionally, if needed. The quantity of pork and molasses can be varied to suit the taste, but the usual proportions are a pound of pork and two table spoonfuls of molasses to a gallon of beans. The beans may be enriched with a small piece of butter instead of pork, or by adding a cup of sweet cream an hour before they finish baking.

BORECOLE OR KALE.

Cook and serve the same as cabbage.

BRUSSELS SPROUTS.

Boil till tender, drain, put in a sauce pan with a little melted butter, season with salt and pepper, simmer a few minutes, and serve on buttered toast; or serve plain.

BROCOLI.

Brocoli bears such a close resemblance to cauliflower that it can scarcely be distinguished from it. Cook and serve in the same manner

CAULIFLOWER.

Wash, trim, boil gently until tender, drain carefully, put in a vegetable dish and dress with drawn butter, or white sauce. The white sauce may be flavored with Parmesan cheese, if liked.

BOILED CABBAGE.

Trim, wash and divide each head into quarters or eights boil till tender, drain, press out the water, and serve with white sauce or drawn butter.

STEWED CABBAGE.

Slice or chop the cabbage, stew until tender, but not soft, drain, add a little sweet cream or milk, simmer ten minutes, and season with salt and pepper.

COLD SLAW.

Slice crisp, firm cabbage very fine, dress with sugar, salt and vinegar; or serve with a French, or cooked mayonnaise dressing.

HOT SLAW.

Slice or chop cabbage fine, stew till tender, season with salt, pepper and butter, add a little vinegar and serve.

SOUR KROUT.

Stew in its own liquor till tender, or fry until slightly brown, in fryings from bacon, or salt pork.

BAKED CABBAGE.

Chop boiled cabbage fine, add milk and beaten egg, season with salt and pepper, put in a buttered baking dish, cover with seasoned bread crumbs and bake brown. Cold boiled cabbage can be used in this way advantageously.

KOL-CANNON.

Chop boiled cabbage fine, add an equal quantity of mashed potato, moisten with milk, season with salt and pepper, mix together thoroughly, and serve hot.

STEWED CELERY.

Cut in inch pieces, simmer until tender in a little water, add sweet cream, season to taste, and serve; or pour over slices of toasted bread and serve hot.

BOILED CARROTS.

Wash, scrape, boil till tender, drain, season with butter, salt and pepper; or slice, and serve with white sauce.

STEWED CARROTS.

Parboil, drain, slice, put in a stew pan with a little broth or milk, simmer till tender, season with salt, pepper and chopped parsley.

FRIED CARROTS.

Parboil, slice, fry in butter till brown on both sides, season with salt, pepper and chopped parsley. Or boil till tender, mash, season to taste, make into cakes and fry brown.

SAVORY CARROTS.

Put in a stew pan three ounces of butter, a tablespoonful of flour, a teaspoonful of minced parsley, half a tablespoonful of minced onion, a grating of nutmeg, and salt and pepper to taste, add a quart of sliced carrots, cook gently–shaking the stew pan frequently––until the contents are a light brown color, then add a pint of broth, cover closely, and simmer until very tender.

BOILED CORN.

Husk, boil till tender, and serve on the cob; or cut the corn from the cob, season with salt, pepper and butter, and serve in a heated dish.

STEWED CORN.

Cut the corn from the cob, scrape off the pulp and eyes, put in a stew pan with a half pint of water to each pint of corn, cover closely, stew gently till thoroughly cooked––stirring occasionly to prevent the corn sticking to the pan and burning––season to taste with salt and pepper, add a little cream or butter, and serve.

CORN OYSTERS.

Split each row of kernels through the middle while on the cob, shave off the corn in thin slices, and scrape out the pulp and eyes. To the corn from each dozen ears add the white of three eggs beaten to a stiff froth and three tablespoonfuls of flour, season with salt and pepper, and fry in spoonfuls in hot fat on a griddle, or in a spider.

CORN FRITTERS.

Beat together till smooth and light, one teacupful of sifted flour, one egg yolk, and half a teacupful of milk, stir in gradually half a teacupful of milk, and two teacupfuls of corn prepared as for oysters, add the white of an egg beaten to a froth, season to taste with salt, and fry in hot fat.

CORN PUDDING.

To a quart of corn prepared as for oysters, add a quart of milk, four eggs, a teaspoonful of salt and a little pepper. Mix well together, pour into a buttered dish, and bake.

CRESS.

The various cresses are usually eaten raw, and dressed according to individual taste. Mixed with lettuce and other salad plants they give them an agreeble pungency.

CUCUMBER SALAD.

Pare the cucumbers, lay on ice or in cold water half an hour, slice thin, and dress with salt, pepper and vinegar. Cucumbers lose their crispness by soaking in vinegar, and should be served as soon as dressed. Their flavor is improved for most tastes by the addition of a few slices of onion.

STEWED CUCUMBERS.

Pare, split in pieces lengthwise, scrape out the seeds, boil five minutes, drain, cover with water, simmer until tender, thicken with flour and butter, and season with salt and pepper. A few slices of onion can be added if liked.

FRIED CUCUMBERS.

Pare, cut in slices of equal thickness, wipe dry, roll in flour, fry brown in hot fat, season with salt and pepper.

STUFFED CUCUMBERS.

Cut off one end of each cucumber, scoop out the seeds, fill with a mixture of seasoned bread crumbs, egg yolk, minced onion and parsley, replace the ends, lay the cucumbers on thin slices of bacon in a dripping pan, pour in a little water, dust with salt, pepper and flour, bake in a quick oven, and serve with brown sauce.

FRIED EGG-PLANT.

Cut in slices half an inch in thickness, lay in salted water an hour, wipe each slice dry, dip in flour or fine corn meal, season with pepper and fry brown in a little hot fat, or dip in beaten egg, then in fine crumbs, and fry in hot lard.

BAKED EGG-PLANT.

Pare, cut in pieces, boil until tender, drain, mash, season with salt and pepper, put in a baking dish cover with bread crumbs moistened with butter, and bake in a hot oven.

ENDIVE.

Endive is generally served raw as an ornamental addition to salads, but may be stewed in cream, brown gravy or butter, seasoned very lightly, and served hot.

LETTUCE.

Lettuce is usually served raw as a salad, and is dressed according to taste, with salt, sugar and vinegar, or with French dressing. It is excellent cooked and served as greens, or as endive.

GREENS.

Brussels sprouts, cabbage sprouts, collards, borecole, endive, spinach, dandelions, young beets, mustard, lettuce, narrow dock, corn salad, purslane, nettles and a large number of other edible plants and weeds are cooked and served in a similar manner under the general designation of "greens." Trim carefully, wash thoroughly, cook till tender, drain in a colander, and season to taste with salt, pepper, butter, vinegar, etc.

HOMINY.

Wash, put to cook in cold water slightly salted, and boil slowly for eight hours, or until tender.

KOHLRABI.

Cook and serve the same as turnip.

KALE.

(See Borecole.)

STEWED MUSHROOMS.

Put in a stew pan with a lump of butter, salt and pepper to taste, and a tablespoonful of lemon juice to each pint of mushrooms, cover closely, stew until tender, thicken with a teaspoonful of flour, add a little sweet cream, and serve.

BAKED MUSHROOMS.

Lay in a baking dish, sprinkle with melted butter, salt and pepper, and bake in a quick oven.

BROILED MUSHROOMS.

Place in a wire gridiron, broil over a clear fire, lay on a hot dish, and season with salt, pepper, butter and lemon juice.

MACARONI.

Macaroni is composed of wheat flour and water, and is simply paste or dough pressed into shape and dried ; but it occupies the anomalous position of being generally classed among vegetables. It is easily prepared for the table, makes a palatable, nutritious and inexpensive dish, and should be more generally used.

BOILED MACARONI.

Break in pieces two or three inches in length, boil till tender enough to be easily mashed with the fingers, drain in a colander and serve with drawn butter, or with white, brown, tomato, or any other sauce.

BAKED MACARONI.

Boil, drain, put in a shallow baking dish, season to taste with salt and pepper, add a little sweet cream or milk, and a lump of butter, cover thickly with grated cheese, sprinkle with seasoned bread crumbs, and bake in a quick oven till nicely browned.

STEWED MACARONI.

Boil, drain, stew in cream, milk or broth, season to taste, and serve ; or serve with any kind of sauce.

MACARONI PUDDING.

Mince together equal portions of boiled chicken and boiled ham, add beaten egg, sweet cream and grated cheese, season with salt and pepper, mix with boiled macaroni, put into a buttered pudding mold, cover closely and simmer in boiling water about an hour; or put in a baking dish and bake in the oven. Serve with any sauce liked.

STEWED OKRA.

Wash and slice the pods, simmer in a little water or broth till tender, and season with salt, pepper and butter.

BOILED ONIONS.

Peel, boil till tender, drain, season with salt, pepper and butter.

STEWED ONIONS.

Peel, boil half an hour, drain, cover with milk, stew until tender, drain, mash or chop, add a little cream, stir until thoroughly heated, season with salt and pepper and serve. Or when cooked tender and drained, dress and serve whole.

BAKED ONIONS.

Peel, boil till tender, roll each onion in tissue paper, bake an hour in a moderate oven, remove the paper, brown the onions, and serve with drawn butter.

SCOLLOPED ONIONS.

Peel, boil till tender, drain, divide each onion into several pieces, place in a baking dish with alternate layers of seasoned bread crumbs, moisten with milk and bake a nice brown.

GLAZED ONIONS.

Peel, slice, put in a baking dish, moisten with brown sauce, or any well seasoned broth, and brown in the oven.

SARATOGA ONIONS.

Peel, slice thin, drop in smoking hot fat, fry till a light brown, drain in a colander, and serve hot.

FRIED ONIONS.

Peel, slice, put in a frying pan containing a small quantity of hot butter or drippings, cover, and fry slowly, turning them over frequently to prevent burning. When tender, and a light brown color, season with salt and pepper, and serve.

PARSLEY.

For flavoring soups, stews, etc., parsley can be minced and sprinkled in them while cooking. For garnishing it can be used raw, or can be put in a wire basket, plunged in hot oil or fat for a minute, drained, and then used.

PUMPKIN.

The old familiar pumpkin is cooked and served in every respect like the winter squash, which is so much drier, sweeter and finer grained, that it has nearly superseded it for table use.

BOILED PARSNIPS.

Wash, boil till tender, drain, cut in slices and serve with drawn butter, or with a white sauce, to which a little vinegar or lemon juice has been added.

STEWED PARSNIPS.

Wash, scrape, cut in pieces, stew tender, drain, press out the water, mash fine, season to taste, add a little cream or milk, and stir over the fire about five minutes.

BROWNED PARSNIP.

Wash, scrape, boil till tender, drain, roll in flour, and brown in drippings or butter, in the oven.

FRIED PARSNIP.

Wash, scrape, boil, drain, mash, season to taste, make into cakes and fry brown.

PARSNIP FRITTERS.

Mash two or three boiled parsnips, add a well beaten egg, two tablespoonfuls of milk, one tablespoonful of flour, season to taste, drop by spoonfuls in a little hot butter and fry brown.

BOILED PEAS.

Shell the peas, tie in a muslin bag, simmer till tender and season with salt, pepper and butter.

STEWED PEAS.

Shell, put in a small quantity of boiling water, cover closely, and simmer until tender. Add sweet cream, a lump of butter rolled in flour, and season with salt and pepper.

PEAS PUDDING.

Soak dried peas several hours in cold water, tie loosely in a bag, boil till tender, rub through a sieve, add half a pint of cream and two beaten eggs, to each pint of peas, season to taste, tie up in a floured pudding bag, boil half an hour, and serve with melted butter, or white sauce.

BAKED POTATOES.

Wash, wipe, put in a moderately hot oven and subject to a gradually increasing heat until perfectly baked, then crack, place in a dish, leave uncovered, and serve hot. The starch in potatoes absorbs moisture when the cells are ruptured by heat, and unless baked or roasted potatoes are broken as soon as cooked. so the steam can escape, they become watery and dark colored, and lose their flavor.

GERMAN POTATOES.

Scoop out, and mash the flesh of partly baked potatoes, mix with finely minced meat, season to taste, replace in the scooped-out skins, put in the oven and bake.

STUFFED POTATOES.

Scoop out and mash the flesh when partly baked, mix with grated cheese, bread crumbs and any other ingredients desired, season to taste, replace in the scooped-out shells and bake.

BROWNED POTATOES.

Pare, parboil, lay in the pan containing a fowl, or roast of meat, and turn over occasionally while cooking, so they may brown evenly.

KENTUCKY POTATOES.

Pare, slice, put in layers in a baking dish, moisten with milk or cream, season with salt and pepper and bake in a quick oven.

Vary the liquid and seasoning used in preparing potatoes according to this formula, and each variation will produce a different dish that can, without impropriety, be named after any State in the Union.

POTATOES A LA ROYAL.

Cut potatoes in balls, parboil, brown in the oven, and serve hot.

Cut in other shapes, parboil, and brown in the same way, and they may be dignified with other pretentious titles.

BOILED POTATOES.

Simmer gently and without interruption, whether pared or unpared, until tender enough to be pierced with a straw, drain, cover with a folded towel and set to dry off, where they will keep hot.

SCOOPED POTATOES.

Cut balls from pared potatoes with a vegetable scoop, boil and serve plain, or with any sauce desired. Old potatoes treated in this way, and served with a white sauce are often imposed upon unsuspecting guests as new potatoes.

STEAMED POTATOES.

Put the potatoes, whether pared or unpared, in a steamer, cover closely, set over a pot of boiling water, and cook till tender.

STEWED POTATOES.

Slice pared potatoes, stew gently till tender, drain and serve with white or other sauce ; or when drained, add a little cream or milk, season with salt, pepper and minced parsley, simmer a few minutes and serve.

SARATOGA POTATOES.

Pare, slice thin, soak in cold water, drain in a colander, dry thoroughly in towels, separate the slices, drop a few at a time into a kettle of hot lard, fry till a light brown, lift with a skimmer, drain on a sieve, sprinkle with salt, and serve hot or cold, as preferred.

JULIENNE POTATOES.

Slice with a crimped, instead of a plain or common, knife, and fry the same as Saratoga potatoes.

POTATOES A LA FRANCAIS.

Cut with a scoop or spoon, and fry in a quantity of hot grease.

PARISIENNE POTATOES.

Cut with a spoon, fry in hot grease and sprinkle with salt and minced parsley.

FRIED POTATOES.

Pared potatoes cut in slices and strips. or in rhomboidal, globular, angular and other irregular shapes and cooked in hot fat are served as Saratoga, Julienne, Parisienne, etc., etc., but however varied the style, and

however fanciful the name under which they **are made**
to do duty, they are simply—*fried potatoes*; and the
secret of frying potatoes successfully—in whatever
shape sliced, or by whatever name dignified—is to have
the lard, oil or drippings at the proper temperature
when they are put into it, and to keep it so during the
entire process of cooking.

BROILED POTATOES.

Parboil, cut in tolerably thick slices, put in a **wire**
gridiron, broil a nice brown on both sides, and season
with salt, pepper and melted butter.

CRISPED POTATOES.

Boil in their skins, peel, place whole in a gridiron,
crisp thoroughly over the fire, and serve hot.

MASHED POTATO.

Pare, boil or steam till tender, drain, dry off, mash
fine in a warm pan or kettle, moisten, to the consistency liked, with hot milk, season with salt, pepper and
butter, then beat very light with a wooden spoon or wire
masher, and serve hot. Be careful to mash the potato
till very smooth before, and to beat it till very light
after, the seasoning is added.

POTATO SNOW.

Pare, boil, rub through a colander, allow the curly
strings to pile up on a heated dish in a snowy mass,
and serve hot.

DUCHESSE POTATO.

Boil, mash, season to taste, add beaten egg, work well, roll out flat, cut in narrow strips two or three inches in length, or squeeze through a pastry bag in shape of lady fingers, and brown in the oven.

CASSEROLE OF POTATOES.

Form an oval pile of mashed potato on a dish, make a hole in the centre the size desired, brush the surface with beaten egg yolk, set in a hot oven till nicely browned, fill the hole with stewed tomatoes, macaroni, or with ragout or stew of any kind, and serve hot.

POTATO CROQUETTES.

Enrich mashed potato with beaten egg yolk, season with salt, pepper, lemon peel, nutmeg, mace or other spices, form into balls or rolls, dip in beaten egg and bread crumbs and fry in hot grease.

SCOLLOPED POTATO.

Fill buttered shells or patty pans with seasoned mashed potato, cover the surface with bread crumbs moistened with butter, and brown in a quick oven.

POTATO PUFFS.

Stir together a cup of milk, two cups of mashed potato, two well beaten eggs, two tablespoonfuls of butter and a little salt, pour into a buttered baking dish, and bake in a quick oven.

POTATO FRITTERS.

To a pint of milk and the yolks of three eggs beaten well together, stir a half a dozen medium sized boiled potatoes grated or finely mashed, and flour enough to make a batter the proper consistency. Add a pinch of salt and the beaten whites of the eggs, and fry in hot grease.

POTATO SOUFFLE.

Put a quart of mashed potato with a little butter, in a stew pan over the fire, season to taste, add gradually half a pint of milk and the beaten yolks of two eggs, stir until the mixture begins to thicken, remove from the fire, add the whites of the eggs beaten to a stiff froth, pour into a baking dish, smooth the surface and bake in a quick oven.

POTATO BISCUIT.

Add a cup of milk and half a teaspoonful of salt to a quart of mashed potato, work in flour until the dough is sufficiently consistent to roll out and cut into biscuit. Bake on a griddle or floured pan. Or a tablespoonful of yeast can be added, the dough set to rise, and when light it can be shaped into biscuit or rolls and baked in the oven.

POTATO AU GRATIN.

Slice cold boiled potatoes, stew in broth or milk season with salt and pepper, sprinkle with grated cheese and bread crumbs, and brown in the oven.

POTATOES POLONAISE.

Stew cold sliced boiled potatoes in broth or milk, and dress with caper sauce.

POTATO A LA MAITRE DE HOTEL.

Stir together in a sauce pan over the fire equal portions of butter and flour, pour in a little milk, add cold boiled potato sliced, simmer till well heated, season with salt, pepper, minced parsley and lemon juice.

POTATO A LA BARIGOULE.

Cut cold boiled potatoes the shape of olives and fry with a spoonful of minced herbs, in olive oil.

POTATO A LA PROVENCALE.

Cut cold boiled potatoes in balls, and fry with a few slices of onion in oil, butter or drippings.

POTATO LYONNAISE.

Cut cold boiled potato in dice, fry, with minced onion, in butter, season with salt and pepper, and sprinkle with chopped parsley.

POTATO BALLS.

Enrich cold mashed potato with egg yolk, make into balls, dip in beaten egg, roll in corn meal or bread crumbs, and brown in a quick oven; or shape into cakes and fry in a little hot fat.

TO STEW COLD POTATO.

Slice cold boiled potato, put in a stew pan with cold gravy or milk, season with salt and pepper, and simmer till thoroughly heated.

TO FRY COLD POTATO.

Slice cold boiled potato, dredge lightly with flour, and fry brown; or fry without dredging.   Or hash fine, season with salt and pepper, and fry brown.

POTATO HASH.

Heat together in a stew pan, a spoonful of butter and a teacupful of milk seasoned with salt and pepper add cold hashed potato, cover closely and simmer gently till well heated.

SWEET POTATOES.

Sweet potatoes are much dryer and nicer steamed than boiled, but are at their best estate only, when baked.   They can, however, be prepared very acceptably, in many of the ways in which white potatoes are cooked and served.   They should be cooked in their skins.

BOILED RICE.

Wash, soak an hour, drain, put in boiling water slightly salted—allowing two and a half measures of water to one of rice—boil till tender, cover with a folded towel, and set where it will dry off and keep hot.

STEAMED RICE.

Wash, soak an hour—allowing three measures of water to one measure of rice—set the vessel containing the rice and water in a steamer, add a little salt, and steam an hour, or until tender. If desired, part of the water may be omitted, and its equivalent in milk added when the rice is nearly done cooking.

SPINACH.

Trim, wash carefully, put in a small quantity of water, cover closely, boil till tender, drain in a colander, press out the water, season with salt, pepper and butter, and serve with poached eggs, or with hard boiled eggs cut in slices; or, after it is cooked and drained, chop fine, put in a stew pan with a lump of butter, add a little sweet cream, season with salt and pepper, stir till well heated, and serve with poached, or hard boiled eggs.

BOILED SALSIFY.

Scrape, cut in pieces half an inch in length, boil till tender, drain, and serve with drawn butter or white sauce; or mash fine, season to taste, add a little cream and serve.

FRIED SALSIFY.

Boil, drain, mash fine, season to taste, add a spoonful of cream and a well beaten egg, make into small cakes and brown on a griddle, or fry in hot fat.

SCALLOPED SALSIFY.

Boil, drain, cut in slices, put in a baking dish with alternate layers of seasoned bread crumbs, moisten with milk and bake brown.

SALSIFY TOAST.

Slice, stew tender in milk, season with salt and pepper, stir in two well beaten eggs, and pour over slices of hot buttered toast.

SEA KALE

Cook and serve the same as asparagus.

BOILED TURNIPS.

Wash, pare, boil till tender, drain in a colander, press out the water, mash fine, season with salt, pepper and butter, serve hot. Or cut in slices and serve with cream sauce, or with drawn butter to which vinegar or lemon juice has been added till slightly acid.

STEWED TURNIPS.

Wash, pare, boil fifteen minutes, drain, add a pint of milk to each quart of turnips, simmer till tender and serve with salt and pepper.

BAKED TURNIPS.

Wash, pare, boil half an hour, cut in thin slices, lay in a buttered pudding dish, sprinkle with seasoned bread crumbs, moisten with milk and bake in the oven until a rich brown.

TOMATO SALAD.

Peel and slice perfectly ripe tomatoes, arrange in a dish, set on ice or in a cold place, and serve plain, or with cream, French, or Mayonnaise dressing. Or arrange on a dish with alternate layers of sliced onions, and serve with French dressing.

STEWED TOMATOES.

Peel, slice, stew until very soft, and season with salt, pepper and butter. Or cream may be substituted for butter, and a delicate flavoring of mace or nutmeg, if liked, can be added. Simple broth or stock of any kind may be used for stewing tomatoes, and a small quantity of onion added for flavoring. The stew may also be thickened, if desired, by the addition of bread crumbs, boiled rice, macaroni, corn starch or flour.

BAKED TOMATOES.

Wash and wipe smooth ripe tomatoes, remove the stems with a sharp pointed knive, place in a baking dish. cook in a moderately hot oven till nicely browned, season with salt, pepper and butter.

SMOTHERED TOMATOES.

Cut in halves, put skin side down in a buttered baking dish, season with salt and pepper, cover with fine bread crumbs, moisten with butter and bake in the oven.

STUFFED TOMATOES.

Make a hole in the centre of each tomato, fill with bread crumbs, season with salt, pepper and butter, and bake.   Or scoop out the inside, put in a sauce pan with some finely minced ham, onion, parsley and bread crumbs, stew fifteen minutes, season with salt, pepper and butter, fill the scooped out tomato skins with the mixture, and bake.

SCALLOPED TOMATOES.

Fill a baking dish with alternate layers of sliced tomato and seasoned bread crumbs, and bake in the oven.

FRIED TOMATOES.

Slice firm unpeeled tomatoes, season with salt and pepper, dip in flour, corn meal, or bread crumbs, and fry until brown.

BROILED TOMATOES.

Slice unpeeled tomatoes, dip in olive oil or melted butter, then in flour or fine bread crumbs, place in a wire broiler and cook quickly.

FRICASSEED TOMATOES.

Slice, fry a nice brown in butter, and lift to a warm plate. Pour a little sweet cream in the frying pan, season with salt and pepper, and turn boiling hot over the tomatoes.

BOILED SQUASH.

Pare, remove the seeds, cut into pieces suitable for serving, put in a covered vessel with a small quantity of boiling water, simmer gently until tender, serve with melted butter, white sauce, or brown sauce; or dry off, mash fine, and season with salt, pepper and butter.

STEAMED SQUASH.

Cut in halves, remove the seeds, steam until tender, scoop out of the skin, and season to taste.

BAKED SQUASH.

Cut in two or more pieces, scrape out the seeds, put in a pan, skin side down, bake and serve with butter; or scoop out of the skin, and season with salt and pepper.

FRIED SQUASH

Pare, steam or stew till sufficiently tender, drain, roll in beaten egg, then in crumbs and fry in hot fat.

SUMMER SQUASH.

Cut in pieces, stew, drain, mash and season with salt, pepper, butter and sweet cream. Or cut in slices, and fry, the same as egg-plant.

SUPPLEMENTARY SUGGESTIONS.

—

Most vegetables can be prepared for the table in a variety of ways; and in a majority of cases, a large number belonging to a special class, can be cooked and served according to the recipes applicable to the preparation of any single vegetable of that class.

By a judicious admixture of two or more vegetables many dishes may be formed that possess characteristics peculiar only to such combinations, and of which the different vegetables composing them are destitute when served separately.

Simmering in broth or plain stock improves the flavor of some vegetables, and "pot liquor," or the water in which ham, pork, corned beef and other salt meats have been boiled, when freed from grease, may be used for cooking vegetables in, if prefered to clear water.

Cooked vegetables need never be thrown away or wasted. They should all be saved and utilized. By skillful re-warming they can be converted into numberless dishes that are attractive and appetizing, and in their preparation can be so varied as to suit almost every taste and fancy.